Publisher's Note

The author suggests you read this book with a pen, pencil or underliner/marker in your hand so that you may make notes and jot down ideas as they occur to you, even write on the pages where and when the ideas occur. As you read this book you will get ideas, lots of them. Jot them down. They will act as triggers to get you going, particularly if you've been thinking along these lines. This book becomes your ledger to the accomplishment of your ideas.

TURNING
HOBBIES
INTO
CASH

C. ANDREW BECK

Library of Congress number 91-077197
ISBN 0-9631520-0-9

Table of Contents

INTRODUCTION

GETTING STARTED

SELECTING YOUR FIRST PROJECT

MARKETING

PREPARING YOUR PRODUCT

YOUR PRODUCT

ADVERTISING

PROJECT FINANCES

PROJECT TIME SCHEDULE

RECORDS AND ACCOUNTING

LICENSES AND LEGAL

INTRODUCTION

Most people that are involved in one or more hobbies did not start out in that hobby with any particular goal or objective in mind, other than an interest. For many people this first small step has led to a varying degree of involvement in that hobby. Some pursue their hobby totally on their own with very little association with others of similar interest. Most hobbyists, however, associate and communicate with others that share their interest.

This association is frequently in the form of participation in hobby activities that are conducted by clubs and organizations. Most clubs have meetings, contests, rallies, etc., that bring their members together to share information about their hobby and for enjoyment. Most clubs and organizations also have various publications on the local, state and national level that provide information for members about their hobby.

Membership in some clubs frequently number in the thousands.

In addition to the tremendous number of club members there are many more individuals that are interested in a particular hobby, sport or activity but do not belong to any formal organizations.

Over the years my wife and I have devoted a considerable amount of time, energy, enthusiasm and money in the pursuit of a variety of interests and hobbies that have not been connected with our livelihood. These "outside" interests have been activities that we do purely for enjoyment such as sailing, skiing, skin diving, model making, photography, etc.--in other words, hobbies. Occasionally we have joined a club or organization that is devoted to a specific hobby in an effort to meet others that share our interests and enthusiasm for a particular hobby.

We are constantly amazed at the number of people that share an interest in a particular hobby. Virtually any hobby you can name has a club or organization that brings together individuals and families that are interested in that particular hobby. Usually these clubs have a local group as well as state and national organizations. Membership in many clubs numbers in the thousands and even tens of thousands on a national level, and some hobby clubs even have international organizations or affiliations.

You undoubtedly have a hobby or, at least, an interest that is shared by many other individuals throughout this great nation of ours. Every year billions of dollars are spent in this country by people, just like yourself, pursuing their hobby for fun and enjoyment. Imagine if you could devise a program to promote and sell a product related to your hobby you would have a business that could be both fun and profitable.

The product, of course, should be something that the other hobbyists that share your interest would enjoy owning. Most hobbyists collect, save, seek out, buy, store and generally accumulate most anything that is directly or indirectly related to their hobby. In other words, they are nuts about the simplest item as long as it reflects their hobbies. Cat lovers will buy calendars with cat pictures on them, model airplane builders will buy drink coasters with airplanes on them, skiers will buy jacket patches with ski resort pictures on them, etc. The list is virtually endless.

Some time ago my wife and I joined a club that brought together people of a particular hobby of ours. This club had sixteen regional chapters throughout the country and also a national organization. The total membership of the entire organization was less than 3000 people. In other words, a very small group. Over the years I was elected to the board of directors of the local group, then secretary, vice president and finally president.

Our club decided to undertake a major national event related to our hobby. This event required that our club provide initial funding that we did not have. Like most hobby and special interest clubs we had no source of income other than dues and membership fees. We constantly searched for ways to increase the size of our treasury to support this national event.

The board of directors decided to put on a calendar project to generate the necessary funds for our treasury. My wife volunteered to be the chairperson of the committee to sell the calendars. Now our calendar was black and white, the same size as dozens of calendars you see at the local store and basically the same as any average calendar with two exceptions.

One, the pictures on the calendars were directly related to the interests of our club and were readily recognizable. Second, special club events were noted on the calendar. In other words our calendar was unique to our club and our hobby.

The project lasted six months and the board decided to print only 500 calendars. The net profit to the club after all expenses and costs were paid was almost $2000. My wife had devoted, on the average, approximately four hours a week on the project while her committee of two did very little. Now $2000 is not exactly something you can retire on the rest of your life, nor is it enough to classify as a full- time business, but when you consider that only 500 calendars were printed and sold to members of a very small organization it was a successful first try.

After the project was concluded, my wife and I discussed the success of the project. Our discussion touched on several points. The project could have been organized better. The cash flow could have been planned so the club would be required to invest very little "up front" money. We could have expanded the project to include clubs with much larger memberships than ours. And the most important, we could have done the project for ourselves and not for the club.

If we did the same project for ourselves and directed the campaign to a club with ten times the membership as ours (and there are many) theoretically we could have made ten times the profit or $20,000. You can see how the number of dollars start getting interesting. Actually on a larger project the profit percentage usually is larger as the cost of your items is usually lower because of volume purchases. The printing costs for each individual calendar is substantially lower when you print 5000 as compared to only 500.

The calendar project was completed five years ago and even today when we visit our club friends throughout the country it is amazing how many still have that calendar. It is, of course, no longer usable as a calendar but it has now become a keepsake among club members and may even become a collector's item one of these days as only 500 were ever printed.

The next project that my wife and I undertook was a coaster program. Special coasters that are placed under drinking glasses were designed and printed. They were sold in sets of one dozen with three different pictures per dozen. We sold them to national and local special interest clubs with memberships much larger than our club. The project is still underway and our profits have exceeded $8,000. We have devoted about six hours per week over the past eight months on this project. An office has been set up in our home and we expect to handle five or six projects per year from our home in our spare time for fun but, most important, for profit.

How will we put on a part-time hobby project? How will we select a project? How will we select an interest or hobby? How will we sell your product? How will we manufacture your product? How? How? Read with us as we answer all of these questions and more in a step by step process. Each step will be fully explored and examined so you may develop your own program to produce a profitable project in your spare time, at home.

NOTES

GETTING STARTED

The first step in getting started with your project is not selecting the project but rather convincing yourself that you do, in fact, want to devote the time and energy necessary to successfully carry through on a project and make a profit. Your project, although hobby oriented, should be selected and developed on a businesslike basis. You should keep accurate records and books, develop a time schedule, a cash flow projection and a budget (all of which will be explained later in this book). Your project, to be successful, should be pursued diligently. You cannot dabble at a project on a hit or miss basis, and expect to succeed. Most important, however, is that if you have received money from someone in payment for goods or services you have obligated yourself to perform. If you do not, you could be inviting all kinds of problems from dissatisfied customers. This is why I suggest you mentally and psychologically prepare yourself to approach your project on a business basis.

There are several methods that you may employ to assist you in mentally and psychologically preparing yourself to succeed.

1. **Business Location**

Set aside a specific location in your home or apartment where you can work and keep all the necessary material related to your project. Your business location need not be a large area, but should be well organized. A desk is preferable, however your notes, schedules and financial records can all be kept in a loose leaf notebook if properly organized. You may have a file or a section in your notebook for each of the chapters in your book and in the same order. The first page in each section should have notes from this book listing the important points of each chapter.

The area in your home that you select should have only the material related to your project. Remove all other material or unrelated items that may tend to distract your attention. The area should reflect your project and should assist you in focusing your efforts on your project. The area should be separated as much as practical from distractions such as the telephone, television and other household activities.

2. **Work Hours**

Set aside a specific number of hours each week that you intend to devote to your project. The actual number of hours may vary as you progress from one phase of the project to the other, however, at the outset you should establish specific hours on a regular basis that you will devote to your project. You may decide that every Tuesday and Thursday you will work on your project from seven o'clock in the evening to ten o'clock.. This will aid you in developing good and consistent work habits but still allow weekends and other times for relaxation and enjoyment, or you may wish to devote a considerably larger amount of time to your project. The intent is to develop projects that are related to your hobby, the advantage is associating a business oriented project with an enjoyable hobby

3. **Project Name**

Give your project a name. This name may change at a later date, but in the beginning the name will be used on all of your project papers, records and references regarding your project. You may prefer to establish a business or company name rather than a project name. Your company or business name will then be the entity that will be developing various projects. The company or business name approach has an advantage in that you may develop several projects over a period of time all under that same name.

Equipment

If you have any business items or equipment such as adding machines, calculators, pencils, file cabinets, staplers, paper punches, etc., place all of these items at your business location. This will further enhance your work area and reflect a more business posture. If you have no business equipment or items then just keep the items you do have at your business location. As you progress through your project you will accumulate a variety of business related items. However, do not run to your local business supply store and invest your money in a lot of unnecessary supplies and equipment. You are operating a business and at the beginning your business has only the money you can afford to loan to it.

5. Business Identity

Post your business, company or project name at your work area. This name should be neatly lettered and placed where it can be easily seen. This will provide you with a business identity. This may appear to be a small item, however, it will serve as another subtle reminder that this is your business location. This is the location where you will focus your attention only on your project. It will also serve as a notice to others in the family that this location is for your project material only.

6. Business Address

Eventually you will need a business address. This address may be the same as your apartment or your home, however, this may be confusing as using this address will mix your business mail with your personal mail. During the beginning phases of your project your home or apartment address will suffice. As you begin to receive product orders or make sales you should change to another address such as a post office box. The reason for this will be discussed later.

7. Your Program

You can develop many more methods to mentally and psychologically prepare yourself to undertake a business project, however, the six items noted above will serve as a good basic starting point.

When you feel you are mentally prepared for your next step, read this book through from cover to cover twice. This reading and re-reading will give you a good overall understanding of the concepts that are presented. After you have read the book, study each chapter in detail and make notes of the important points in each chapter. From your general notes you can begin to develop your own written program for proceeding with your first project. Review your notes to see if they agree with our summary. Your written program need not be lengthy or exceptionally detailed but you should include the following points:

1. Your hobby or special interest.
2. Your proposed project.
3. Your research and development.
4. Your marketing and sales program.
5. Your time schedule.
6. Your project budget.

These items are the basic points of any project and should be written down. You may modify your program several times as you proceed, but it is most important to start with a written document outlining your proposed program.

NOTES

SELECTING YOUR FIRST PROJECT

Once you have assembled the basic office materials, defined your work area, your work hours and outlined your program, you are ready to define your first project.

In the back of this book are two lists for your review. The first list "Hobbies or Interests" gives you nearly 300 headings that will assist you in defining those hobbies or activities that you most enjoy or which have special interest to you.

3. The First Project

Examine the list of hobbies or interests and make special notes of those items that appeal to you the most or of which you have particular knowledge. Possessing some knowledge of the hobby or interest in your project is important. The more knowledge or experience you have in a particular area is helpful. If you pursue a project that is related to classic automobiles, as an example, it is important to know something about classic automobiles. If you are interested in classic automobiles but have no real knowledge of them it will be necessary to schedule a research period in the time schedule of your project. Keep in mind that when you begin your marketing and sales program you will be appealing to many people who probably know much more about classic automobiles than you do, so you had better know something about classic automobiles.

After reviewing the list of "Hobbies or Interests" in this book, you should then make your own list of those particular hobbies or interests that appeal to you the most. Your list may have fifteen to twenty items, or even more. Now review your own list and group those hobbies or interest that are similar. As an example, aerospace, aircraft, airplanes, avionics, classic aircraft, flying, gliding, model airplanes, outer space and soaring are all somewhat related hobbies or interests. Your own list may be further refined to define the specific hobby or interest that form the starting point for your first project.

It is entirely possible, and I might add, desirable to develop a specific interest that may appeal to more than one organization. An item incorporating vintage airplanes in it, as an example, may find a market with airplane clubs, flying clubs and model airplane clubs. This, of course, greatly broadens your market potential and sales volume.

You may select a hobby or interest that has not been shown on the list in this book. This is fine as long as the hobby or interest is something you will enjoy and pursue diligently. Actually you could select any hobby and develop a successful project. However, if that hobby is one that you sincerely enjoy, your success rate should be higher.

9. The Product

The next step necessary in developing your project is to select an item to sell. Begin by examining the list of projects at the back of this book. The list has a brief explanation of each item to assist you. Naturally, you may not necessarily select an item on the list, but select an item you would enjoy making and selling. The selection of the product is most important and must be carefully considered. First of all, the item you select should have as much appeal as possible to as many potential buyers. It must be an item that a large number of people can use themselves or an item that would make an attractive gift. Decide how the item you select for sale can be adapted or modified to appeal to the special interest or hobby group that you have selected.

As an example, let's assume that your hobby or interest is flying and your flying activities are recreational and you fly private single engine aircraft. A wide variety of items such as ash trays, book marks, calendars, drink coasters, letter openers, placemats, etc., etc. may be produced with pictures illustrating single engine private aircraft. Whichever item you select would then be attractive to fellow pilots, single engine airplane owners, flying club members, model airplane enthusiasts and many individuals that just like airplanes. Therefore, one product would have potential sales to several market areas.

Assuming you have selected the product you intend to manufacture and special interest area that you intend to sell your product to, determine how to design, manufacture and sell your product.

NOTES

MARKETING

Your marketing and sales program is, without a doubt, the most important part of your project. Your product must sell or you do not make any money. It's as simple as that. Of course, the better product you have the easier it will be to sell. Marketing and sales programs will always be the keys to your success. Your marketing program must be thoroughly thought out and planned. Research your market area and determine the size and location of your market. Who will buy your product? Where are they located? How many customers can you expect? How do you contact the greatest number of people? What price will people pay for your product? Should you sell through clubs, organizations, publications or on your own? Should you sell to organizations, retail outlets or to individuals? We will explore all of these questions in this chapter to assist you in planning your marketing and sales program.

Research

I have found that the best place to begin your research is at your local library. Using the periodical index file you can compose a list of periodicals that are currently being published regarding specialized areas of interest. These periodicals and magazines are an excellent source of contacts for your marketing program. Most popular hobbies or special interest have one or more magazines published for that one area of interest. There are car magazines, flying magazines, surfing, photography, model, etc., any of which could provide sales potential for your new product.

11. Mail Order

It is important to note that the majority of your sales may be through "mail order." This simply means that most of your sales may be by the use of the mail system and most of your products may be delivered to your buyer through the mail or other delivery system. To do this your advertisement for your product will be placed in a magazine, club bulletin, newspaper or other such printed publication. Your buyer will read the advertisement for your product and forward their order to you through the mail. When you begin to receive orders for your product you will supply your product to your buyer through the mail or other similar type of delivery system.

First, prepare lists of magazines that may be of interest to potential buyers of your product. As an example, if your product has a theme based on flight or airplanes you could research flying magazines, model airplane magazines, possibly some travel magazines and even general model magazines. If the library has copies of these magazines you can study them on your visit to the library. Study carefully the magazines to determine how heavily oriented it is to your area of interest. Would the typical reader of that magazine be interested in purchasing your product?

Examine the advertisements in the magazine-- is there competition, what kind of ads do they have? When you find the magazines that will appeal to potential buyers of your product, write down the name and publisher. You can then go to your local news stand and purchase a copy for further study. When you study your magazines turn to the publisher and advertisers pages (usually in the front of the magazine) and note the advertising representatives location, the publisher and the circulation. You can contact the advertising representative and request a copy of their advertising rates card and their fees. Also find out their deadlines for publishing advertisements as well as the type of material and the form of the advertising copy. Most publications require that you submit your ad copy two to three months prior to actual publication.

Many magazines will have sections for club news or will list clubs that are in existence for the purpose of bringing together individuals of a common interest. Start a list of such clubs or organizations. along with their addresses. Contact these clubs to see if they have publications for their members. Because many of these publications carry advertisements at reasonable rates. The important point is that these publications are directed to readers of very specific interests.

Many of the publications cannot be purchased at the local news stand as they are so specialized. The circulation of these national or local club publications is usually much smaller than general area interest magazines you can purchase at the news stand, however, your sales vs. circulation percentage is usually much higher.

A good example of the above would be the marketing of a product that was oriented to a particular breed of horses or dogs. There are animal magazines on most local news stands with circulation in the tens of thousands. If you are selling a product with an appeal to owners of Arabian horses or Doberman Pincer dogs and you advertise in an animal magazine, your sales ratio will probably be very low. On the other hand, if you look for magazines that are normally not on the local news stand such as Equis and Horse Illustrated which are for horse owners or the American Kennel Gazette, Popular Dog and Dog World which are for dog lovers, these magazines have smaller circulations, but your sales ratio will be better. A specialized product that is advertised in a publication of the same specialization will be attractive to the readers of that publication.

Additionally, if you advertise in the Arabian Horse World or the Doberman Pincer monthly and you are selling a product oriented to Arabian horse owners or Doberman dog owners, the total circulation will be lower still but the sales ratio will be very high. The important point is to do the research to determine what publications are available. There are dozens of special interest publications that never appear even on the most extensive news stands. Therefore this is a very important part of your research program.

13. Membership Lists and Rosters

Membership lists and rosters of members of special interest or hobby clubs and organizations can be an excellent source to assist in your marketing program. A good product at a reasonable price should help to produce a higher percentage of sales to members. Your method of advertising to these members may require a considerable amount of attention, work and expense as the only way to contact all members on the list is to send an individual personalized advertisement to each member. This requires the printing of hundreds of advertising "flyers" and then you must address and mail all those flyers.

On the calendar project that I noted earlier, approximately 3,000 flyers were hand addressed, stamped and mailed. That was a lot of work but the calendars sold well. A high sales ratio was realized which was worth the extra effort.

Perhaps you are presently a member of a club or organization that you may be using in your market program. If you are not presently a member of such a group, you may investigate the possibility of joining such an organization to assist you in developing your marketing program. I certainly do not advocate or encourage you to join an organization club or group for the sole purpose of making money off of your fellow members. You should join a group primarily to further your knowledge and experience and to meet people with interests or hobbies similar to yours.

If after you have joined a club or group you determine that your fellow club members would be interested in purchasing your particular product, then you could develop your marketing program around your club. Should you decide to use your club, group or organization as the basis of your marketing program obtain copies of your national, regional and local membership rosters. You should then determine which publications are most frequently read by your fellow members and also if there are one or more club publications.

Of course it is entirely possible to obtain this information without necessarily joining a group, club or organization. This may be difficult and will require contacting club members for a copy of membership list or roster. However, it should be pointed out that the purpose of this book is to assist you to develop profitable projects from your present hobbies or interests. Therefore, you may enjoy your interest or hobby more if you elect to join a special interest club or group oriented to your hobby.

The important point of your marketing is to structure a program to contact the greatest number of individuals that will be interested in purchasing your particular item. Marketing is partially a function of your product, of course, but more than likely your product is designed to appeal to club members, which is usually a rather small group of potential buyers.

Automobile and soap manufacturers advertise in many general interest magazines with very large circulations because generally everyone must have an automobile or soap, etc. If you are selling calendars featuring Persian cats you will do far better to advertise in publications oriented to Persian cat lovers. If you advertise calendars featuring Persian cats in an electronics magazine you may be wasting your time and money. Always consider your market and the readers of the magazine that carries your ads.

14. **Retail Market**

When you develop a product that has an appeal to a relatively diverse market, you can contact representatives of chain retail outlets.

The retail store you select should be a chain-type company. In other words, a company that has more than just one store. A chain retail store will likely require a high volume product, meaning you must sell a rather large number of your product to generate any real profit for them and yourself.

To sell successfully through a retail store begin by selecting stores that have many locations in several cities. Contact the head purchasing agent for that retail chain. It's advisable to see that individual in person after you have made an appointment. It is very easy for any business person to ignore or throw away a letter. It is nearly as easy to dismiss someone on the telephone. However, if you meet someone in person and you have a good product that can generate a profit for the store, you stand a good chance of getting a contract or at least a trial order.

When you approach the owner of the local sporting goods store, and sell him on the idea of displaying your product, he may say OK. However, if he has only one store, he may only sell a few of your products each week plus he will expect something for his effort and this reduces your profit margin.

Your product should have a rather universal appeal to a large number of people such as skaters, skiers, bicycle riders, joggers etc. There are many people from children to the elderly that enjoy these types of hobbies and sports and never join a club, organization or group of any type. Also many joggers never buy a jogging magazine, many cyclists never buy cycling magazines. But these people frequently visit retail stores that specialize in merchandise for joggers, cyclists, skaters, etc.

Secondly, if you request an appointment the secretary will usually ask the nature of your business. If you are then given an appointment after explaining your business, it indicates they may be interested in your product.

Several points must be made regarding sales through a retail chain. You must review your project budget very carefully to determine at what price you can sell your product to the retail store and still make a reasonable profit for yourself. Keep in mind that the retail store must in turn sell you product at an attractive price and also make a profit. So you must be prepared to discuss price to the purchasing agent.

Also you must know your production capabilities and when you can realistically deliver your product. You certainly don't want to develop a super product and have it enthusiastically accepted by a purchasing agent who then presents you with a contract for 10,000 items of your product with a 10-day delivery schedule.

So be well prepared in advance of your meeting. Know your product, know your costs and know your production capabilities.

Generally speaking, a mail order or direct marketing campaign is usually the best way to get started. If this approach proves successful you can then branch out into other marketing programs.

There are a variety of books and magazines on the market that discuss marketing concepts and philosophies. You may wish to visit your local library to review this material. Appendix A on page 103 lists several books that are available in many libraries.

NOTES

PREPARING YOUR PRODUCT

The first step in preparing your product is to resolve in your own mind the type of product you intend to produce and sell.

There are unique features to each and every product you may choose to produce. All products will require some form of design. Calendars, placemats, coasters, bumper stickers and similar products will require art work or photography. You should have some knowledge of these types of art forms or at least know someone that will provide assistance in this area.

Projects such as lapel pins, earrings and key chains will require some knowledge of jewelry design and manufacturing. The point is that you should feel confident that you can produce a product that will reflect sufficient quality to appeal to prospective buyers.

15. Product Definition

I personally have very little knowledge of jewelry or how jewelry is manufactured. I, therefore, would not feel particularly comfortable attempting to produce a product of this type. If my research indicated that an attractive pair of earrings, as an example, would have a large sales market for a particular hobby or special interest group, I would seriously consider a project of this type. I would either associate with or utilize the advice of someone that is knowledgeable about jewelry design and manufacturing. I do not feel that I could produce a design for earrings of sufficient quality to attract buyers. I would rely on others to assist or work with me on the design of this particular project, you may feel the same.

The product you select to design and produce should be an item that you like, you would enjoy owning or that you would appreciate receiving as a gift. Enjoying what you do is a most important factor in determining your attitude with which you approach your product. An enthusiastic, positive attitude is a decided asset in the success of your project. So if you develop a product that you feel comfortable with and you will enjoy designing and producing, your chances of success are greatly enhanced. Not only should your monetary rewards be greater, but your self-satisfaction level will be much higher.

You may develop an excellent design for a matchbook that would appeal to a particular hobby club or special interest group, however, if you are a non-smoker there is a very real possibility that you will not approach the project with as high a level of enthusiasm as may be necessary for success. If you are a poor cook and consider dining out to be the local fast food hamburger stand then it is reasonable to suggest you not attempt to produce and sell a cookbook. You probably wouldn't know where to start and your success percentage may be quite low.

We have found that you should select a product that you feel comfortable with and will enjoy working on. When you are confident that you have selected the product that satisfies these requirements next determine what kind of a market you can expect for the sale of such a product. This will require research.

In defining and preparing your product you may want to evaluate the interests and the type of individuals that are involved in your hobby club or interest group. If your hobby is boxing, motorcycles or guns it is reasonable to assume that your potential buyers will be primarily men. Therefore, it would be wise to not select earrings, cosmetic kits or jewelry boxes as your product. These same products, however, would be acceptable to hobby clubs or groups interested in antiques, baking, cosmetology and dressmaking as the membership is predominately women.

16. Pricing (Also see Section 21 and 24)

The sales price level of your product is also related to your hobby or interest group. Hobby clubs such as yachting and private aircraft owners would be inclined to purchase items that may be more expensive than other hobby groups. Products that have a sales price that are in the $5 to $10 range are readily acceptable to most hobby club members. Products priced over $25 will be much more difficult to sell unless they are very unique and of high quality. All of these factors are important in selecting and preparing your product.

A good way to start is by carefully examining similar products that are already on the market. You may wish to purchase similar items so that you may study them in detail although you can usually study these products in a store in sufficient detail without purchasing.

You should make notes as to the size, price, content, quality, manufacturer and the type of sales outlet. You may even ask the store manager how many of the particular item is sold per month. If the item is advertised in a publication you should clip out the ad for examination and reference. Many items are offered for a 10-day free trial basis. If so send for the item, examine it and send it back. If you can't do this you can send a letter requesting more information on the particular item being sold.

If you do your research in sufficient depth you should have a good idea of what your product must be to sell. You should know the quality, price and general design variation of your competition. Then if you can produce a similar product of comparable quality and price with design emphasis on the hobby club or special interest group of your choosing, you should have a potentially successful product.

17. Product Testing

Test your proposed product on your friends, hobby club members or acquaintances in your special interest group. Discuss, generally, your proposed product with them to determine the level of acceptance of your idea You may have a design of your product to show them, perhaps even a mock-up or proto-type. Most people will give you an honest reaction as to their impression of your product. When you are in the home or office of your friends and hobby club members, you should look around to see if they have similar products. If they do it is a good indication that they may be interested in purchasing your product.

When you have developed a sketch or design of your product, visit with the managers of local retail stores to discuss the acceptability of your product. Products oriented to dogs, cats or pet lovers may be discussed with local owners or managers of pet stores. By expressing interest it is a reasonably good sign that you have created an acceptable product.

The design of your product may be truly unique and unusual. It may be a product that does not exist on the market. To protect such a design, you may wish to discuss your product with a patent or copyright attorney.

If you cannot find similar products in stores or advertised in magazines and you get negative reactions when you discuss your product with friends, acquaintances and retailer, you may want to re-examine your product. With no similar products available, either you have a great unique and new idea or you have a product that no one sells because no one wants it. When you discuss your new and unique product with your friends and acquaintances they say they don't like it and would not consider buying one, then you may want to consider looking for another product.

Large national manufacturers devote considerable amounts of time and money in the research of new products and market areas. You do not have that luxury and must, therefore, rely on your own marketing and research. The procedures outlined above are not particularly scientific, but they do produce a degree of results in that they either prove or disprove the market appeal of your proposed product. To proceed without some degree of market research is certainly not advised.

NOTES

YOUR PRODUCT

18. Product Design

While price and the acceptability of your product is very important, the single most important factor in the appeal of your product will be its design. A well-conceived design in itself will be a large asset in selling your product.

You begin your design by carefully considering the individual that will be purchasing your product or the area that your marketing program is expected to cover. As discussed earlier, your product will be specifically designed to appeal to a particular hobby club, organization or special interest group. Carefully examine that club, organization or special interest group to determine the specific design theme for your product.

As an example, let's assume that you will be producing and selling coasters to place under drinking glasses or, perhaps, calendars. Secondly, let's assume that you will be selling these coasters or calendars to owners and lovers of classic automobiles. You will probably want to illustrate classic automobiles on your coasters or calendars. First, research the automobile industry to determine which model automobiles are, in fact, classics. From the list of classic automobiles note the American classics and foreign classics. Of all classic automobiles there are some that are considered to be all-time great automobiles while others, although classics, are not great designs. So you should determine which designs are the really great designs as defined by true classic automobile authorities.

From this select list of classics you may then select the actual classic automobiles that you will be illustrating on your coasters or calendars. After you have gone through all of this then locate the best photograph or drawing of the automobiles you have selected. Remember you will be selling these coasters or calendars to buyers that probably know more about classic automobiles than you do. So it is important that you select true classic cars to illustrate on your product.

Follow this same basic procedure for any of the projects you select if it involves a particular distinct item, such as airplanes, boats, dogs, horses, etc. as opposed to general hobbies such as fishing, hunting, etc. If your project involves an interest group that is more of a sport than a hobby you will probably not be involved in a selection process as outlined above. Sports oriented projects appealing to jogger, surfer, hang gliding, etc. do not always have items that can be classified as classics necessarily.

Many products such as key rings, note pads, tie pins, credit card holders, hat emblems, etc. will have only a single design that reflects your hobby or special interest. This design must be easily recognizable and attractive. A well done outline of a dog, bird, flower, tennis racket or golf club defines those particular hobbies or interest. The design may be more involved than a simple outline but it may not necessarily be a classic design. The name of the club or the hobby may be desirable along with other types of graphics.

19. Special Events

You may wish to develop a product to communicate a specific event or date of an event. This product could be a hat, T-shirt or emblem that would illustrate the hobby along with the date of a specific show, rally, event or meeting. This particular type of product will only be attractive to buyers during that particular event. You may sell some items after the event as mementos or collector items but the majority of your sales will be at the event itself, or prior to the event.

Begin the actual design of your product with the product itself. Will you be using an existing product and adding to it? Will you be using a product that is currently in production and modifying it? Or will you be designing an entirely new product? Let's examine all of these alternatives.

0. Modify an Existing Product

There are a wide variety of items that are offered in gift shops, stationary stores and other retail outlets that may be used as the base of your product. These would be items such as brushes, calculators, cigarette lighters, clocks, desk clocks, flashlights, hats, jewelry boxes, sewing kits, etc. These and many other items are currently in production. By simply adding a logo, outline, embossed figure or medallion that reflects your hobby or special interest you have a product that is unique and will be attractive to your hobby club members or your special interest group.

Purchase a sample of the product from a store to use as the base for your product design. Then you should produce a mock-up of the log or medallion that you intend to use and apply it to the item. You now have a proto-type of your product that you propose to sell. Show the proto-type to your friends and potential buyers to get their reaction as to the acceptability of your product. If it appears that your product is well received proceed further with your program.

If you decide that your product will be a modified version of an existing product you should proceed as in the previous example. Visit gift shops, hobby shops, stationary or retail stores to locate the type product you have chosen. Products to be modified may include billfolds, bookmarks, Christmas ornaments, first aid kits, license plate holders, photo albums, posters, umbrellas etc. When you have selected the particular product proceed with the design modifications to make the product unique to your hobby or special interest group.

The next step for either modifying an existing product or adding to an existing product is to locate the supplier of the particular base product. Some retail outlet store managers may give you the name of the company that supplies them a particular item. If they do not look for a trade name or company name on the product you have chosen. This may require some research and telephone calls to locate a local manufacturer of the product that you have chosen. There are also companies that specialize in supplying a wide range of business, professional and personal gift items that may be tailored to a specific need.

Once you have located the company that may supply the basis for you product you should contact the company, preferably in person. At the meeting you should discuss design of the finished product and how to best accomplish your final product. The company representative should provide some assistance, particularly if you are modifying an existing product. Key rings, mugs, clip boards, billfolds, notebooks, ornaments, desk calendars, paper clip holders, stationery, greeting cards, etc. are only a few of the existing products currently on the market that may be modified for your specific use and design. The manufacturer's representative will supply you with all the information you need such as quantity of items, colors, delivery method and schedule and, of course, cost.

4. Adding to an Existing Product

Adding to an existing product or modifying an existing product is a rather easy way to produce your first product. Your main responsibility in developing the product will be the design or the modification or addition itself.

When you modify an existing product or add to an existing product work with the manufacturer to obtain the best possible price. If you can locate more than one manufacturer, it's a good idea to obtain competitive bids for the same quantities and quality.

In adding to an existing product or modifying an existing product very little of your time will be involved in the manufacturing process. This is obviously a time saver but it usually will affect the sales price and your profit margin. As an example, let's say you decide to sell a rather good quality key holder that incorporates the logo of your hobby or special interest club on it.

A manufacturer may offer to supply you with 2000 modified metal key holders for perhaps $1.75 each. Not a bad price for a well done quality metal key holder. However, a retail price should be 4 to 10 times the price that you pay for the manufactured item. This is not always true, but it is a good rule of thumb. Using this rule you should sell the key holder for $6.50. You must examine this price very carefully to determine if your fellow hobby or special interest market will pay that price for your item. Also is the price competitive with a similar product currently being sold. If similar key holders without the custom logo can be purchased for $4.50 you may have a problem. Hobby or special interest buyers will usually pay more for an item with their special hobby illustrated on the item but they may not pay $6.50 for nearly the same key holder that sells for $4.50 at the local store. So examine your production and price structure very carefully.

22. **Manufacturing a Product**
     The third method of producing a product is where you act as the manufacturer. This will involve more time on your part and also require some design abilities. Products that you could manufacture would be bookmarks, bumper stickers, calendars, cross stitch

patterns, drink coasters, picture frames, placemats, etc. These products will require that you do all the design, conceptual and final drawings or at least collaborate with an associate that has these talents. A calendar or drink coaster project are good examples of this type of project. When the final designs for those items are completed you need only to secure competitive bids from local printing shops to print your product. You may wish to consider the copyrighting of your design prior to exposing your product to others.

The cost to produce the calendar project that I mentioned in the Introduction was $1.28 per calendar. Our sales price was $5.25 per calendar. This is a sales price of approximately four times our actual cost. Our sales price for an attractive wall calendar of $5.25 is certainly competitive with a similar calendar that may be purchased in any local store. The calendar project is an example of a good product at a fair price. However, projects such as a calendar require substantially more effort and talent on your part, but the potential rewards are higher. Our calendar project required that we do all the art work and coordination. Also a calendar project is seasonal as you have only the months of November and December to sell the product.

NOTES

ADVERTISING

You may be selling some of your products through mail order by advertising in publications for your hobby or special interest club. Sending an advertising flyer to club members or advertising in a hobby-related magazine are good methods of selling your product.

3. **Your Ad**
Any advertising media you use will require that you first prepare the ad "copy." This is the actual advertisement that will appear in the magazine, flyer, newspaper or whatever source you select. Most advertisers require that you submit your ad exactly as you want it to appear in their publication. Black and white is the easiest to prepare and is the least expensive to reproduce. On the other hand, black and white will not attract the attention that will an ad with some color. Your ad must be brief, easy to read, to the point and eye catching. This is not as easy as it may sound. You may wish to consider the services of a professional that can assist you with your ad. A poorly designed, un-

professional ad can do your project more harm than good.

The advertising representatives of many magazines offer professional ad designs as part of their services. If you do not feel confident with your own design abilities you may wish to work with a professional.

State in your ad, as simply as possible, what you're selling, how your product may be purchased, and for how much. Your ad should be eye catching to the potential buyer. A photo or drawing of your product is desirable to clearly show the special interest or hobby aspect of your product. If your product has a cat on it to appeal to cat lovers, then the cat should be clearly visible and should dominate the ad. This will catch the eye of the potential buyer and they will read your ad. The ad copy should briefly explain your product. Try to keep the explanation around 25 words or so. Buyers are reluctant to read ads that go on and on or rambles.

24. Single Pricing

Of course, your ad should simply and briefly explain how the buyer may purchase your product and for how much. Often successful ads have included a small printed coupon that may be cut out and mailed to the seller. This coupon has space for the buyer's name, address and how many of your products they wish to purchase. Also clearly show your address complete with zip code. It is, of course, important that you include the price in your ad. The advertised price may be an all-inclusive number to avoid any mathematical computation on the part of the buyer. In other words, advertise a price that includes handling, postage and sales tax in addition to the cost of the item. In this way there is no mathematics required on the part of the buyer and there is no confusion. If you advertised the price of an item, then expect the buyer to add the cost of postage and sales tax you may receive a confusing array of computed prices. So the best thing is to offer one price in the ad with no add-ons or "post paid."

The exception to this single pricing philosophy is if you have a product of which a buyer may wish to purchase more than one item. You then may wish to offer a "price break." As an example if you are selling an item for $3.95 each including tax, postage and handling you may offer to sell three for $10.00 including tax, postage and handling. This will save the buyer $1.85 and will probably save you more than that in postage and handling and record keeping expenses. This, of course, will depend on your product. Some products will be suitable as gifts, others will be items that have multiple uses and functions and a buyer may wish to purchase more than one. Some products lend themselves to single purchases. So decide which category your product will fit into as it will effect your marketing program.

5. **Tax and Postage**

The major portion of your sales may be through mail order. If this is the source of some of your sales it will be necessary to include the cost of postage in the price structure of your product as stated earlier. If your product price is fixed and the cost of postage is added to that price your ad becomes more complicated, however, your buyers are treated more equally in terms of the cost of postage.

All of this is a minor consideration if you are selling your product in a rather small geographic area as the postage will be relatively constant. However, if your sales are over a wide geographic area such as several states, the postage will vary greatly by area and product size.

Whichever method you utilize it is strongly suggested that you take several of your products that are individually wrapped for delivery, to two or three local post offices. The postal clerk will weigh and compute the postage required to deliver your product to several destination points that you suggest. The reason that you take several of your products to two or three post offices is that the costs will vary. That may surprise you, but it happens more often than not. If you take one of your products to one post office you will be told the price to mail your product to a given destination point. Then a week later, you take another of your products to the post office and the cost will more likely than not be different. So always check the price of several of your products at two or three post offices, then figure the average price in your advertisements. Research the postal rates carefully.

Sales tax must also be carefully researched particularly if you sell your product out of state. Sales taxes often vary from state to state and in some states the tax will vary within that same state. Again decide if the sales tax will be included in the overal price of your product or as an add on.

26. Classified Ads

In addition to the advertising strategies outlined above, there are a variety of magazines that have classified ad sections. Many of these ads are selling items similar to yours and can be seen month after month. The advantage of this type of advertising is that the cost is usually much lower than a large specialized ad. Also it is not necessary to prepare the ad copy with special graphics, photographic or illustrations. There is no designer involved in preparing this type of ad. All that is required is a typed note simply stating your product, the price and where to send the money for your product. The disadvantage to this type of ad is that it will not be as easily noticed as will the larger ad that is illustrated. The larger ad will usually generate more sales than will a small classified type ad. however, you can usually purchase 4 to 8 small classified ads for less than one large ad. It is a difficult decision to make and one that may require some actual testing.

If you will be developing your first project on the minimum of investment, you should consider the small classified ad approach. This will keep your initial costs down until you have generated sufficient funds to use more sophisticated advertising techniques. Your sales will be less dramatic and you will be ordering your products in smaller quantities, perhaps 500 or less at a time. The effect will increase the unit cost of each item which will reduce your profit margin. So you must carefully analyze your financial position to determine which procedure will be best suited for you. Keep in mind that every project has an element of risk so controlling your front end cost or financial exposure is important. It may be best to use the small ad and start small until you generate operating capital then you can expand into more ambitious and larger projects.

Keep in mind that hopefully you will be building a long term, on-going successful business. Therefore, if you are operating on a "shoe string" you may wish to start small and learn the procedures of producing a successful project even though you may not generate a large profit. You should then plan each succeeding project to be larger than the previous. You should also be in a position to manage and operate each successive project more successfully.

27. Ad Check List

All of the above guidelines are intended to assist you in drawing a profile of your potential purchases. Then design your ad program to match this profile as much as possible. Your buyer profile will be developed partially during the development of your product. In other words, you should have a reasonably good idea of your buyer before you determine completely what your product will be.

In preparing your ad remember these important points.

1. Do not exaggerate.
2. Be truthful.
3. Deliver the product as noted.
4. Show a delivery time schedule.
5. Price of your product.
6. How the product may be purchased.

7. To whom the check or money order must be made out (usually the manufacturer)

8. Address.

9. What to do if not satisfied.

10. Is your offer limited.

11. Brief description.

12. Endorsed by _____.

The important aspects of a mail order ad campaign to achieve maximum results are: the right offer, the right ad, the right product, the right media and the right records. Your ad records will assist you in determining which ads produce the best results.

What is said in your ad is more important than how you say it. The main appeal in every ad should be benefits. Before your buyers will order your product they want to know what it will do for them. Next in importance is news. A new product or a product that has made news is exciting and buyers want to read about it.

Remember your buyer is not familiar with your product and wants to know everything there is to know about your product. Long ad copy is much preferred over short copy when describing your product and its benefits.

NOTES

PROJECT FINANCES

If your project is not a profitable venture then, obviously, there is no point in proceeding. So the planning of your project financing is of extreme importance. In this chapter we will examine all aspects of your project financing and help you develop as complete an economic picture of your project as possible. We will examine your cash flow, product pricing and your overall budget as well as some suggestions on organizing your books.

A serious word of caution is in order at this point. All projects are not financial successes and there are no guarantees that you will make a profit, so financial planning is of extreme importance.

28. Consideration

The financing of your project will be a factor in determining the type of product you will be manufacturing and selling. If you have very little personal funds to put into your project, you will want to plan your project so as to require as little "front end" money as possible. If your project requires a large amount of front end costs, you may have a problem. If your project requires front end money that you do not have you may wish to form an association or partnership with a friend that can contribute some financial support or financial partner. If you do this you will be sharing your profit with your partner. You may be able to borrow money, but interest is usually required. Sharing your profit with a financial partner or paying interest on borrowed money will reduce your potential profit.

Unless you have excellent credit standing or good relations with your bank it will be most difficult to finance your project through a lending institution. The main reason is that your project has no security or equity that is of interest to a lender. Also, if for some reason your project does not generate a profit, you will then repay the loan from your own funds. Also when you repay your loan you pay interest on the money which will reduce your profit.

Let us begin with a structure that finances your project in such a way as to require a minimum of dollars up front.

29. Up Front Expenses

The "up front" expenses are generally defined as the moneys that will be necessary to start your project and keep it going up to the time you begin to sell your product. Another way to explain your finances is in terms of cash flow. Cash flow is either negative or positive. Your project will generate a negative cash flow until you receive enough sales money to reach your "break even" point. Then your cash flow will enter the positive side of the ledger. The break even point is reached when your sales income equals your expenses. From that point on your project should generate a profit.

30. **Cash Flow**

A word of explanation about "cash flow." At the outset of your project you will be spending money for such items as research, supplies, telephone and a variety of other project expenses. Your product will not be ready for sales so you will have no income from your project. During these early phases of your project your money (cash) will be flowing out of your business account, creating a negtive cash flow. Your expenses will be larger than your income. As you begin to sell your product, money (cash) will begin to "flow" back into your business account as your receive income. When the amount of your income equals the amount of money you have spent for expenses you will reach the "break even point." Now as you receive additional income from more sales your "cash flow" become "positive" and you begin to realize a profit from your project.

Some or all of the above terms may be new or even confusing to you unless you have some business background. To an accountant or businessman these terms are part of every-day business vocabulary. Regardless of your background, we will proceed with the assumption that you have no accounting or business background.

31. List Costs

The first thing to do is prepare a list of items you will need and tasks to be performed that will cost money. Everything you do that is remotely related to your project is to be accounted for in detail. There are two basic reasons for this. First, know the total number of dollars you are spending on your project so you can sell your product for enough money to recover all of your expenses plus a reasonable profit. Second, know your total project costs, your total sales and your profit so you may accurately report the entire financial statement to the Internal Revenue Service and other taxing agencies. Yes, you pay income tax on the profit from your project. You will be required to pay self-employment tax, state and local tax on the profit of your project. So be certain that you account for every penny and have records and receipts.

To assist you in developing your budget we will list items that you may need in addition to the actual cost of your product and the sales program. Keep in mind that you should keep your expenses to a minimum and purchase only those items that are absolutely necessary. Don't assume that you are going to make a lot of money on your project and proceed to buy a lot of expensive equipment and furniture such as desks, typewriter, calculator, etc. Once you have made a profit on your first project you may choose to spend some of that money on furniture and equipment for your future projects.

Here, then, is a list of items you will probably need to begin your project.

1. Calendar for marking your critical dates on your schedule.
2. Pencils and note pads.
3. Notebook with dividers.
4. An accounting record book or accounting paper to put in your notebook.

The list is short, but actually that is all you will need to get started. now as you go along you may wish to acquire additional items, but the above is a list of the basics.

2. **Budget**

Now let's take a look at your budget. First of all let's make a list of those items that will cost you money to complete your project. After we have listed these items we will examine the budget items in more detail.

Expenses
1. Supplies.
2. Equipment.
3. Licenses and fees.
4. Legal fees.
5. Telephone.
6. Office.
7. Utilities.
8. Publications and subscriptions.
9. Membership fees.
10. Automobile and travel.

11. Entertainment.

12. Postage.

13. Advertising.

14. Manufacturing costs.

15. Research and development.

Supplies are basically the items listed on the previous page. You may wish to print stationary or business cards, paper clips, stapler, etc. These are all items that will be supplies or, more specifically, office supplies. Supplies are normally items that will be used up during the course of your project.

Equipment is items such as typewriter, calculator, adding machines, pencil sharpeners, etc. In other words, items that are not used up or consumed during the course of your project. We recommend that you do not purchase these items for your first project as you can usually manage a successful project without this type of equipment. Secondly, you cannot arbitrarily show the purchase of equipment as a project expense for tax purposes. Your equipment is usually depreciated over a period of time.

33. Fees

Licenses and fees are occasionally charged by some cities to acquire a business license. Check with your local government to determine what licenses or fees you are obligated to obtain.

Legal fees and accounting fees. If you choose to use a fictitious name for your business, or if you choose to form a corporation or a formal business you may want to consult your attorney. If your project is expensive or if the finances are complex you may wish to consult with an accountant. If so, these legal fees must be accounted for. Generally speaking, you will probably not require these professional services on your first project.

34. Other Costs

Telephone. You more than likely have a telephone where you live which is probably used for personal calls. When you begin to use this telephone for business purposes you may wish to charge some of these expenses to your project. Keep accurate records and a log of which calls are for business purposes.

Office expenses are the costs you would incur if you maintained an office for your project. More than likely you will not have office expenses at least for your first project as you will probably handle everything from your present home or apartment. If you maintain one room in your home or apartment you may, under certain circumstances charge a portion of your household expenses or rent to your business. Before you do, be certain that you review this with your accountant or the person who prepares your tax returns.

Utilities are much the same as your office expenses outlined above. These, however, will include your electricity and possibly gas and water. These expenses will be extremely small unless you are maintaining a separate office.

Publications are an important item although usually not a large cost. There are books, magazines, newspapers, club bulletins, etc. that you will be purchasing for your project. Some of these publications may be in the form of yearly subscriptions for magazines oriented to the field of interest that you will be appealing to for your marketing program. Also, the cost of this book can be included in publication costs.

You may choose to become a member of one or more clubs or organizations during your project or in preparation for your project. The membership costs, fees and dues should be charged to your project.

Some travel will be required during your project. There will be trips to the post office, stationary store, your supplier's office, etc. You should keep accurate records of the date, destination and the miles you have traveled. If you use public transportation, keep track of that also. Your auto travel expenses should be computed in cost per mile. You may wish to assign your own cost per mile number for your own records, however, IRS will only allow so much per mile for tax purposes. Again, check this out with your tax man.

Entertainment is a cost to your project when you are entertaining someone for the specific purpose of promoting or developing your project. This is a very touchy area and sometimes most difficult to define. Be certain that you state, the location, date, name of the individuals involved, the nature of the business conducted and, of course, the expense.

Postage is somewhat self-explanatory and will involve the mailing costs of anything that has to do with acquiring information, memberships, publications, etc. for your project. Now if you use mail order to sell your product or if you return your purchased product to the buyer by mail, these mailing costs will be part of your manufacturing costs.

Advertising costs will include everything that is required to prepare your ad or flyer and have that ad published in newspaper, magazines, club bulletins, etc. Any artwork, photography, art supplies, etc. will all be advertising costs. If you receive assistance from a artist, designer, photographer, etc. these costs will also be advertising expenses. The fee charged by magazines, newspapers, club publications, etc. will all be advertising expenses.

35. Manufacturing Costs

Manufacturing costs will include the actual cost to produce your product whether you purchase a completed product from a manufacturer or purchase a variety of components and assemble them yourself. If your project requires assembling prior to delivery to the buyer and you employ others to assist you, these costs are part of manufacturing. Packaging for mailing your product will be manufacturing costs. Any costs that relate to completing this product and delivering it to the buyer is a manufacturing cost. If you employ others to assist you in any phase of your project it should be on a contract basis where the employee is an independent business person. If individuals that assist you are employees it is necessary to deduct for taxes, workman's compensation, state disability, etc. Before you employ anyone you should discuss this matter with your attorney and your accountant.

Research and development will be any costs you incur to learn more about your product or your marketing area. It is possible you may be required to travel to a conference, seminar or function of some form to research your project. Again be certain you keep careful and precise records of all of your expenses.

The above budget items are usually associated with larger projects or businesses and are listed to illustrate the type of expenses you may incur at some time. However, if your first project is somewhat modest and you wish to proceed cautiously, your budget will not include all of the items above. It must be pointed out that we do recommend that in your first project you do proceed cautiously and keep your project small and uncomplicated.

36. Budget Planning

Earlier in the book we mentioned a very small calendar project that we conducted several years ago. To illustrate the preparation of a calendar project, we will use the general numbers and cost items that we encountered on that project except we will assume a sales market of 5000 calendars instead of only 500 that we actually decided to sell. In this way you should have a realistic model of a small project to use as a comparison for your project. Keep in mind that your project may have additional costs and expenses and the costs themselves may vary.

Supplies - pencils, paper, eraser, $ 25.00
paper clips, etc.

Equipment - we borrowed an adding machine from a friend	-0-
Licenses and fees - we had membership in a local and national club that comprised our market area.	35.00
Legal Fees -	-0-
Telephone - we assumed we would have approximately $15 a month telephone expenses for six months	90.00
Office	-0-
Utilities	-0-
Publications and subscriptions 3 magazines for one year	42.00
Automobile - assume 200 miles per month at .18/mile	36.00
Entertainment	-0-
Postage - letters of inquiry, mailing subscription, members, etc. $20/mo. for 6 mo.	120.00
Advertising - Full page ad in one club magazine and two 1/4 page adds in two other magazines for a six month period, plus 80 flyers to each of 16 regional clubs for distribution to their members.	75.00
Cut of the 12 photos used in the calendar The art work for the calendar and all mock-up work to make the calendar "camera ready."	185.00
Manufacturing costs - the printing and binding of 5000 calendars.	3750.00
Calendar mailing costs at .40 each	2000.00
Research and development - Attendance at four club functions	40.00
Total costs to produce and prepare for delivery of 5000 calendars	$ 6398.00

This is a cost of $1.28 per calendar

We reviewed many calendars at the local stationary store, gift store, etc. and determined that we should be able to sell our calendars, because of their special appeal to the organizations, for $5.25 each including postage, handling, etc. Therefore, our projected profit was as follows:

Sales price 5000 calendars at $5.25 each =	$ 26,250
Cost to produce 5000 calendars =	6,398
Gross profit	$ 19,852

Note that the term "gross profit" is used. This is because the taxes have not been deducted. The reason is that the tax on the amount will vary if you are an individual, a corporation, or whatever form you have for your business. Your income bracket will affect the tax.

37. **Financial Planning**

When you look at the budget for the calendar project, your first reaction will probably be: "$19,852 is a nice profit, but I certainly can't afford the $6,398 to produce the calendar in the first place." Of course very few people can. What we must now do is what is called "cash flow planning." What will be your cash requirements for your project and at what point in time may actually be required to spend the money.

The total cost of the calendar project is $6,398. However, only $613 is required to totally prepare the calendar and complete your advertising campaign. The balance of $5,785 will not be required until it is time to deliver the calendars to the buyer. Most printing companies will be more than happy to work with you on scheduling the completion and delivery of your work. So in the case of our example calendar project, meet with the printer and review your "mock up" calendar with him. If your work is satisfactory he will give you a price to print 1000, 2000, 3000, 4000 or 5000 calendars. The more calendars he prints the less will be the cost of each individual calendar. Your printer will also give you a delivery schedule, usually two to three weeks.

At this point you do not order the printing of your calendar. You leave the mock-up with the printer and get a receipt along with a copy of your agreed pricing schedule.

The next step is to begin your advertising campaign in which you include a notice to your buyer to allow 4-6 weeks for delivery of their calendars. At this point you can do little more than wait for the magazines to be published with your ad. When the magazine is published you should begin receiving your orders.

If you have a six months ad campaign for 5000 calendars you should receive at least 1000 orders during the first month as subsequent months the quantity of orders tends to taper off--not always, but usually. If you do receive a 1000 orders in your first month you will have received $5250 (based on a sales price of $5.25 per calendar). You have now recovered your original $613 investment and have an additional $4.637. You should now have enough money to purchase 1000 calendars to send to your first 1000 buyers.

You may wish to order 2000 or the full 5000 calendars assuming that by the time you actually take delivery of the calendars from the printer you will have an additional 500 to 1000 orders. You should plan the ordering of your calendars so that you have enough money on hand from your buyer to cover the purchase price from the printer plus packaging and mailing.

Near the middle of your six months marketing campaign you may experience an increase in sales. The reason is that your earlier buyers show their new calendar to their friends who in turn decide to purchase one or more of your calendars. If during the first 4 to 6 weeks of your marketing campaign you receive 200 to 300 orders, you will probably not sell the 5000 calendars you had estimated. In that case it will require a longer time to recover your original investment and you may sell only 1000 to 2000 calendars.

If you do not sell nearly as many calendars as you originally expected you must carefully review your program to determine why you were not as successful as you had expected. Review your marketing program to determine if you reached the potential buyers that would really be interested in your product. Was the quality of your product high enough to justify the sales price? Was your ad professionally done and did it have eye-catching appeal? You should ask yourself all of these questions so as to improve the performance of your next project.

If your project is successful and you sell all of your products you have done a good job and should compliment yourself. However, if you did not generate the profit that you had expected you may wish to examine your pricing structure. The pricing is a very important aspect to the success of your project. Your project costs can be determined rather accurately and you should know precisely the unit cost of the product you are selling.

The pricing, or unit sales price of your product, is an entirely different matter. The price of your product is entirely up to you and you can literally name your own price. Obviously if you establish a very low price for your product you should have little problem selling your product, but you will generate very little profit. On the other hand, you can set a rather high sales price that would create a considerable profit if you were to sell all your products. But you may price yourself out of the market. Meaning that you have established a sales price so high that no one will buy your product and your project will be a financial disaster. So the pricing of your product is extremely important.

You must balance the pricing between a reasonable sales price for value received and price at which the competition is selling. The product you sell will very likely be very similar to other products already on the market. The difference is that your product has a unique appeal to a special interest group of buyers as we have discussed earlier. For that unique appeal buyers are usually willing to pay a premium or higher price than similar products without the unique appeal. They will pay more but not a great deal more. They certainly will not pay double the price of comparable products. They may pay 10% or perhaps 20% more at the maximum. However, if you can produce your product and sell at the same price as your competitors you should be successful because of your unique feature and your marketing program that is appealing to your hobby or special interest market group.

Your production costs and your total project costs must be kept to as low a level as practical. You must work diligently to reduce your costs in all areas but not at the sacrifice of quality. Your buyer must receive a product that justifies the sales price. This is particularly important to you as a businessperson. Good quality for a reasonable price is somewhat rare in today's market. You will, hopefully, have other projects and other products as time passes. Also you may be selling to the same or similar market areas or buyers.

Therefore, if you establish a reputation for selling a good product at a reasonable or competitive price, it can be a big step in assisting your success in future projects. On the other hand, if you sell inferior products that are over priced you could be heading for trouble. So research thoroughly your competition both from a quality point of view as well as pricing structure.

38. Record Keeping
In the preparation of your project you should keep reasonable records of your time. You should know how much time you are devoting to your project, for two basic reasons. When you have completed your first project, it would be interesting to know how profitable your project was on a per hour basis. If you made a $5000 profit on your project but devoted 2000 hours of total time to the project you would have earned $2.50 per hour. This kind of profit is not very exciting. So it is a good practice to keep accounts of your time.

The second reason that you should keep your time records is to compare your first project with subsequent projects. Your first project will usually be the most difficult and time consuming as you will be learning the ropes and becoming familiar with the procedures and business practices. Your first project should be profitable but will also be a learning experience. On future projects your management procedures should be smooth and more efficient. You will undoubtedly develop procedures of your own.

PROJECT TIME SCHEDULE

A very important aspect to your project is your time schedule. The scheduling of your first project will be difficult because you probably have very little knowledge as to how long it will take to accomplish a particular task. Also you may be optimistic regarding how much time you will actually devote to your project. You may say that you can devote two or three hours per day to your project. You can turn off the television and devote that time to your project. This will work fine for three or four weeks, then you may find yourself drifting back to diversions such as TV and other interests. Therefore, schedule your program and establish goals and milestones for yourself rather than attempt to devote a fixed number of hours to your project.

39. List Tasks

The first step in developing your time schedule is to list the basic tasks to be performed. Once you have developed this list, attempt to assign a number of days that you realistically can expect to accomplish that particular task. After you have assigned days to each of the tasks, it will be a simple matter to superimpose those days on a calendar. You can then mark the completion date of each task and thereby establish "target" dates.

Your schedule can be adjusted and altered as you proceed, but you should attempt to adhere to your schedule as much as possible. If you begin to miss your target dates and allow your schedule to slide, you will develop bad business management habits and your project will suffer. Keep in mind that you are in total control of your project and the success or failure of your project is entirely up to you and how efficiently you administer your affairs. The development and maintaining of your time schedule is good business practice.

There are, of course, some aspects of your time schedule that will not be entirely under your control. If your product will require printing or some form of manufacturing process, you may be obligated to work within the time schedule and work load of the company that is doing the printing or the manufacturing of your product. Your advertising campaign will probably include publishing your ad in a magazine or newspaper. Magazines and newspapers have publication deadlines and lead time. Some magazines have lead times of two or three months. Also most publications have the right to reject an ad for a variety of reasons. So if it is critical that your advertising program begin on a certain date and you miss a deadline and must wait for an additional two or three months, it could kill your program.

A calendar program is an excellent example. Most people buy calendars in November, December and some in January. Before November very few people are very concerned about next year. After January most people already have a calendar and will not be interested in purchasing a calendar for that particular year. So you really have a sales period of only about three months. Not only is this a brief sales period, it is a period that cannot be adjusted. Begin your sales program in November. If you begin your sales program in any other month, particularly later, your project can suffer.

40. Seasonal Scheduling

Projects that are oriented to a particular season or event will also require careful timing. A project for the Christmas season must be ready for sale in November or December. If you do not have your product ready until January, you are in trouble. However, a seasonal project, unlike a Christmas ornament, can always be sold the following year. Calendars are only good for one year.

Your total schedule, then, is of extreme importance. Total schedule is determining starting and ending time as well as the functions during the project. You will "fine tune" your project schedule as you acquire additional information during the progress of your project.

41. Delays

Unforeseen delays are usually more common occurrences during the course of a project than are events that will save time. So your schedule should attempt to foresee potential delays. This is difficult to anticipate, you must allow some time for rough spots in your project. It is most difficult to develop a "tight" schedule and at the same time allow for unexpected time delays.

One way is to discuss your project in detail with others who you expect to assist you in producing your product. These individuals would include artists, copy writers, magazine publishers, postal officials, manufacturers, printers, photographers, etc. These are individuals who may be involved in your project and their work load, production schedules and deadlines can affect your project schedule as much as the actual time they will be working on your project.

A photographer may determine that he will need two weeks to prepare photographs that may be necessary for your project. You then program the two weeks in your schedule for the photographer. Several weeks later when you ask the photographer to begin work on your project you may find that he has scheduled a month vacation for himself and can't touch your project until he returns.

A printer may tell you in March that he will require three weeks to print your 2000 calendars. In October you take your calendar mock-up to the printer for printing and discover that he has committed to printing a large order for another customer and can't print your calendars for two months. This type of unforeseen time delays can kill a project and cost you considerable loss of time and money.

42. Involving Others

Your schedule is, therefore, very important to yourself but also to others that may be involved in your project. During the research phase of your project you will be discussing various project items with others. During your discussions you should get a good general idea of how long they will require to work on your project as well as what their expected work load should be when they will be starting your work. If possible, you should get a tentative commitment from as many of your "vendors" as possible.

As you get more information on your schedule you can firm up many of your dates. As this occurs you should continually contact your photographer, printer or whoever will be working with you to guarantee that they can, in fact, perform for you within your time schedule.

No time has been shown for the receipt of sales orders, the manufacturing time and the packaging and delivery time as this period will vary greatly and will depend upon the success of your marketing program and the design of your product.

It cannot be stressed strongly enough how important your time schedule will be to the success of your project. The main reason is that the time schedule will give you a continuing series of target dates to accomplish a designated task in your project. This should be one of your prime motivating tools to keep your project moving ahead. So you must prepare a realistic time schedule and stick with it.

43. **Typical Schedule**
Above all, remember that schedules usually require more time than you originally programmed. It is rare that a project is produced in less time than was scheduled.

Suggested Project Schedule

Task	Time
1. Study of this book and list desirable projects.	4 weeks
2. Select interest area and define program	3 weeks
3. Initial project research and selection	3 weeks
4. In depth research of market area.	6 weeks
5. Preliminary project schedule.	2 weeks
6. Begin design of project.	6 weeks
7. Prepare preliminary project budget.	2 weeks
8. Finalize marketing program.	3 weeks
9. Finalize project schedule.	2 weeks
10 Prepare advertising copy.	3 weeks
11. Receive bids from manufacturers.	2 weeks
12. Finalize project budget.	1 week
13. Establish project sales price.	2 weeks
14. Begin sales program, submit ad to publisher.	3 weeks
15. Receive sales orders from buyers.	--
16. Direct manufacturer to proceed with product.	--
17. Package and deliver product to buyers.	--
Total Time	42 weeks

RECORDS AND ACCOUNTING

As you proceed through the various phases of your project it is important that you maintain accurate and complete records of everything you do for several reasons. Your records will provide a good history of your first project and will be most helpful on future project. This history will assist you in defining which aspects of your project were the most successful and which aspects could be improved upon. Your records should include your marketing concepts, who you contacted and why. Your records will document the important decisions you have made along with the results. Your original time schedule and budget from you records can be compared to the final time schedule and budget.

Your Records

Your records should include the names, addresses and telephone numbers of all the individuals that you contacted during the course of your project. This will include friends, club members, organizations and most importantly all of the vendors or suppliers that you contacted for goods, services or bids on various portions of your project.

If possible you should obtain business cards of the individuals and/or companies that you contact during the evolution of your project. Company brochures are also important to save. You may not utilize the services of a particular company or individual on your first project, but you may consider that person or company on a future project.

45. Keep Notes

It is good business practice to write everything down as soon as possible. This would include important decisions, actions, dates, conversations with individuals both in person and on the telephone. Never rely on your memory, keep written notes.

The best way to keep records and notes of conversations and daily items is to use an inexpensive secretarial notebook. Note the date on each page, then keep a brief log of your basic activities and your personal or telephone conversations. As your project progresses you will find yourself reviewing your notes many times. When your project is completed your notes will provide a complete day to day history of all of your activities during the course of your project. These records will be very important in the preparation of your program for your next project.

46. Financial Notes

Your financial records are most important and must be carefully maintained. Any and all prices that are quoted or discussed by vendors, suppliers or individuals must be in writing or at least noted in your records books. You will be surprised at how often a verbal price quote will vary from the actual contract price. So get it in writing or write it down yourself.

It will be necessary for you to account for everything you spend on your project as well as every cent you receive. Your financial records are extremely important. You project finances are the final determination of the success or failure of your project. Each and every expense must be recorded by a paid receipt or check accompanied by a written explanation of the reason for the expense.

7. Checking Account

You may wish to open a separate checking account for your project to assist you in maintaining your financial records. A separate checking account will assist you in maintaining accurate financial records. As you purchase items related to your project a separate checking account will avoid mixing personal expenses with business expenses.

. Accounting

The best way to maintain your financial records is to buy an inexpensive three column accounting notebook. Standard three column account notebooks have a column to record the date, a column to note the purpose of the expense (or income) and the individual. Also there is a column for the check number itself. Then the three right hand columns are for expense, income and account balance. Each and every amount of money that you invest, loan, spend or receive on your project must be noted. Along with you notations in your financial record book, you should keep a file of all back-up information for each expense such as receipts, canceled checks, estimates, proposals, etc. All of this material is important to your first and future projects. Your thorough review of all your records will be most important in planning all of your future projects.

Please keep in mind that you will be investing your own money on your project and at some point in time your project will return your investment. Therefore, you must keep accurate financial records.

49. Financial Reporting

Maintaining accurate financial records of your project is extremely important for the financial success of your project and also for tax reporting. You must report any and all income to the Internal Revenue Service and also to your state government. Your reporting method will depend on the method of structuring your project in terms of legal definition.

On your first project you will more than likely report your project financial records on an IRS-1040 Schedule C for Business Income or under "Other Income." As you develop more and more projects you may wish to operate under some form of company or corporation, in which case you should consult with an accountant and perhaps an attorney.

The scheduling of your project may be a factor in planning your finances. Your financial records will probably be based on a calendar year as is the case with most of us. We typically pay our taxes based on our income from January 1 through December 31 of each year. It is entirely possible that you may have a six month project that could start in September of one year and end in February or March of the next year. The first three or four months of your project would probably be the period that incurred the major portion of the expenses. The last two or three months of the project would experience all of the income from the project. In this situation your project may generate a financial loss for one year and a profit for the next year. Again your financial records along with accurate dates are important.

NOTES

LICENSES AND LEGAL

The purpose of this chapter is to point out the various licenses you may be required to obtain and some legal questions you may wish to consider. We are not offering legal advice as we are not attorneys, however, there may be legal aspects to some of the projects you may wish to undertake.

50. Business License

Most cities require a business license for any and all forms of businesses. In most cities a business license is rather easy to obtain and reasonably priced. It is advised that you contact the City Clerk's office of your city to inquire about the business requirements for the city in which you will be doing business. Usually it will not be necessary to obtain a license until you begin your advertising and sales program. You may not need the business license during the research, marketing and manufacturing phases of your project.

You may also wish to discuss your proposed business with the Planning Department of your city. If you operate your business out of your home or apartment you may be required to obtain a home occupation permit. If, however, you use a post office box in a commercial zone as your business address you may not be required to obtain a home occupation permit. We strongly recommend that you discuss your proposed project with your local city or county office to determine the licenses or permits that may be required.

51. Fictitious Name

The use of a fictitious name on your projects is something that you may wish to consider. A business name or company name usually appears more professional than using your own name. Many vendors or subcontractors may feel more comfortable if they feel that they are working through a business rather than an individual.

If you elect to use a fictitious name for your business it is important that you investigate the use of the particular name that you select to be certain that that name is not currently being used. In most areas it is rather easy to investigate the use of a name. In California you contact the local office of the County Clerk. This agency has a form and procedure for reserving the use of a business name. A form is available and a name search is involved as well as a modest fee.. The reservation of your own business name is important as you could have a problem if you use a name that is already reserved. If you wish to open a business checking account your bank will require evidence of your reserved business name.

52. Corporation

Forming your own corporation may have some advantages such as the ability to purchase items by use of a resale license, which has tax advantages. However to incorporate a company is an involved and expensive process and should be handled through an attorney. For your first few projects the expense and procedure involved in forming a corporation greatly exceed the advantages. It is, therefore, not recommended that you incorporate at the outset. You may wish to discuss incorporation with an accountant or an attorney after you have successfully completed several projects.

53. Patents

Patent infringement is an area that you may consider in the development of your product. Many of the project items listed in the appendix of this book may be purchased from suppliers. Also many of the items are manufactured and/or sold by a wide variety of companies. Many of the items either do not have patents or are not the type of item that may be patented or issued copyrights.

If you purchase an existing product for resale or a product that you intend to modify and resale you should check with the supplier regarding any possible patents on the item. In most cases it will not be a problem, but it should be clearly understood at the time of purchase that you intend to resale the product you are purchasing or that you intend to modify the product and then resale that item.

If you manufacture a product yourself you may wish to consider possible patent or copyright infringements. Many of the items on the list in the appendix either may not be patented or are issued a "design" patent. A design patent is issued by the U.S. Patent Office in Washington D.C. on the specific design of an item as opposed to the use or function of the particular item. If you produce an item that basically fulfills the same function as an item already on the market but has a distinct design variation, you are probably not violating any design patents

If perchance you do sell an item that may infringe on an existing patent you may receive a letter from the attorney of that patent holder requesting that you discontinue the sale of your product. It is high unlikely that you will produce a product that will infringe on an existing patent, but it is always wise to discuss this issue with your supplier.

It is entirely possible that you may design a truly unique product that does not now exist on the market and has a wide commercial appeal. In this case you may wish to consider filing for your own patent on your product. Filing and obtaining a patent is a lengthy process and involves expense and we recommend you work with a competent patent attorney.

54. An Unhappy Buyer

The last subject in this chapter is the unhappy buyer of your product. You may possibly have a buyer at some time during one of your projects that may be unhappy with you or your product. If the buyer has received a defective or faulty product you must be prepared to refund the buyer's money or send the buyer another of your products. Your response to an unhappy buyer should be prompt, businesslike and courteous. Above all you should document all sales and refunds.

If your sales are through a form of mail order system you must specify a time schedule for delivering your product. Typically in mail order forms you will see a note such as "allow 4 to 6 weeks for delivery." You should include this type of a note in any and all advertisements that involve some form of delivery schedule. The time schedule must be realistic and you must be able to deliver the product within the time frame that you specify. A word of caution, if the delivery time is inordinately long, it could very well adversely affect sales.

Remember all buyers are valuable customers even though they may be unhappy with their first purchase. If all buyers are treated respectfully, courteously and promptly, they may purchase future products from you and may refer their friends to you. Make every effort to satisfy your buyers. Offer to refund their money if they return the product that they purchased.

NOTES

CONCLUSION

Now that you have read the book you should have a good basic understanding of the concepts presented. These concepts should help prepare you to undertake your first of many successful projects based on your hobby or special interest.

In assembling this book we have attempted to present the subjects of each chapter in a logical sequence. However, all of the subjects are so closely interrelated that the sequence is secondary. The information presented in each chapter is of course the most important aspect of the book. As you proceed with your project you will find yourself referring back and forth to all of the chapters as opposed to methodically proceeding from one chapter to the next.

The concepts presented in this book are good basic business procedures that have been oriented to producing a product based on your hobby or special interest. We have developed and completed successful projects based on the concepts in this book so we are confident that the basic business approach is sound and does work.

We have attempted to present in this book a program that is easily understood and based on sound basic business principles. This book, however, only offers the program; the real success of your project is up to you. The success of your project will be directly related to how diligently you develop and pursue your project. .

Good luck on your first and on your future projects.

APPENDIX A

<u>WHERE TO ACQUIRE ADDITIONAL BUSI-NESS INFORMATION</u>

There are many places to obtain information about starting a small business. The following information should be helpful.

<u>Small Business Administration</u> - Local offices are listed in the telephone directory or contact: office of Public Affairs, Small Business Administration, 1441 L St. NW, Washington, DC 20416, (202) 653-6832. Ask for a list of publications, prices and ordering information.

<u>Service Corps of Retired Executives</u> - S.C.O.R.E. - Check your local directory or contact National S.C.O.R.E. Office, 1129 20th Street NW, Suite 410, Washington, DC 20036. This is an excellent source of practical and useful information.

<u>Trade Associations</u> - Join one or more of these associations relating to your business. Most have Trade Shows at least once a year. Try to attend as

many as possible to become aware of new products and trends.

Service and/or Professional Organizations - Membership in these organizations is excellent for networking. Usually your local Chamber of Commerce will have information about one or more of these groups. Contact several of these groups, get their literature and visit with them before you decide which group is the one you want to join.

United States Chambers of Commerce - Contact your local chapter or the national headquarters, United States Chambers of Commerce, 1615 H St. NW, Washington, DC 20062, (202) 659-6000.

Internal Revenue Service (IRS) - Contact your local branch office or Taxpayer Information and Education Branch, Taxpayer Service Division, IRS, Department of the Treasury, 1111 Constitution Ave. NW, Washington DC 20274, (800-234-1040).

Social Security - Contact your local branch or call 1-800-234- 5772.

State Board of Education - Check your local directory for your state's number, (if applicable).

Local or County Library - An excellent source of free information. Your librarian will assist you in obtaining desired publications and information. This is a good way to review a publication or book before purchasing for your personal library.

Community Colleges - Most community colleges have business related courses in either their regular classes or through the Extension or Community Service divisions. A good way to acquire needed information, at a reasonable expense, and be able to have questions answered as needed.

State Universities - An excellent source for gaining information. Their libraries are also a valuable asset. Courses are usually more expensive than those at a community college. Many universities have an Extension Division that frequently offers certificated programs that may be taken at your speed. A certificate is awarded instead of a degree.

Trade Journals, Magazines - This is a good way to be aware of changes, trends, new materials, new suppliers of materials required to produce your product.

Suggested reading from your local library.

Start and Run a Profitable Home-Based Business by Edna Sheedy, published by International Self Council Press, Inc.

Advertising and Sales Promotion: Cost effective techniques for your small business by William H. Brannen, published by Prentice-Hall.

Advertising Pure and Simple by Hank Seiden, published by American Management Association.

Successful Direct Mail Advertising and Selling by Bob Stone, published by Prentice-Hall.

Street Smart Marketing by Jeff Slutsky, published by Wiley Publisher.

Marketing Tactics Master Guide for Small Business by Gerald B. McCready, published by Prentice-Hall.

Good Idea! Now What?: A friendly guide for bringing your idea from birth to bonanza for evenless than a little money by Howard F. Bronson, published by Bestsell Publications.

Marketing without Advertising by Michael Phillips and Sally Rasberry, published by Lolo Press.

Do-it-yourself Marketing Research by George Edward Breen, published by McGraw-Hill.

APPENDIX B

The following is a list of potential products that may be developed for your project. The majority of these products will have your hobby name, logo or emblem on the item.

Address Numbers - House numbers printed or carved in/on metal, plastis or wood.

Ash Trays - Glass, metal or plastic ash trays.

Balloons - Packages of balloons of various colors.

Belt Buckles - Metal belt buckles.

Belts - Leather, plastic or woven belts.

Billfolds - Leather, plastic or fabric billfolds.

Bookmarks - Heavy paper, cardboard or plastic bookmarks.

Bottle Opener - Metal or plastic bottle opener.

Bracelets - Metal or plastic bracelet of various colors.

Brushes - Plastic or wood handled brushes of various designs.

Bumper Stickers - A wide range of bumper stickers can be produced with club graphics.

Business Card Holders - Metal or plastic business card holder, pocket or desk version.

Calculators - Hobby name or logo on the calculator itself or the holder-case.

Calendars - A wide range of calendars can be produced with hobby photos, special interest photos and club dates.

Candle Holders - Ceramic, metal, plastic or wood candle holders with hobby name or logo or the holder itself in the shape of the hobby interest.

Candy - Boxed or wrapped candy of various types with hobby name on the box or label.

Can Opener - Metal can opener with hobby name on the handle.

Cast Figures - Figures cast of metal, plastic or ceramic depicting the hobby.

Charms - Cast or molded metal or plastic charms for bracelets or necklace.

Christmas Ornaments - Cast, carved or molded metal, plastic, glass or wood.

Cigarette Lighter - Purchased lighter with hobby name, logo or emblem added.

Clip Boards - Clip boards in various colors.

Clocks - Wall or desk clocks.

Collars - Pet collars of leather, plastic or fabric.

Combs - Personal or pet combs.

Cookbook - Book of recipes.

Cosmetic Kits - The cloth or plastic kit container for cosmetic items.

Compass - Purchased compass for key chain, auto or boat with hobby name.

Credit Card Holder - Plastic, leather or fabric folder for credit cards.

Cross Stitch Pattern - Specially designed pattern with club logo.

Cuff Links - Cast metal, ceramic or plastic cuff links.

Decals - Printed window or other surface decals of various colors or designs.

Desk clocks - Purchased clocks with hobby name applied.

Dice Game - Dice with plastic or leather container.

Drink Holders - Plastic or metal drink glass holders for autos or other vehicles.

Earrings - Cast metal, ceramic or plastic earrings.

Eye Glass Retainers - Fabric or leather eye glass retainers with neck strap.

Eye Glass Case - Fabric or plastic eye glass carrying case.

Fingernail Clippers - Hobby name or logo applied to fingernail clippers or carrying case.

Fingernail Files - Metal or board files with hobby logo or name on the file or carrying case.

First Aid Kits - Kits with minor medical supplies.

Flashlight - Purchased flashlight of various sizes.

Floor Mats - Plastic or fabric floor mats with hobby name or logo.

Greeting Cards - Various greeting card designs.

Grocery Bags - Paper, cloth or plastic grocery bags.

Hat Emblems - Cloth or plastic hat or coat emblems.

Ice Scrapers - Plastic or metal ice scrapers for windows.

I.D. Tags - Plastic or metal identification tags for pets, children or key rings.

Jackets - Club or hobby name, logo or emblems applied to front or back of a jacket.

Jacket Patches - Similar to hat emblems but designed for jacket or shirt pockets.

Jar Openers - Plastic friction lid openers.

Jewelry Box - Wood, metal or plastic jewelry boxes.

Jewelry - Wide variety of jewelry items can be produced with hobby characters.

Kites - Paper, cloth or plastic kites.

Knife - Carving knife with hobby name, logo or emblem applied.

Key Chain - Metal or plastic key chain or holder.

Labels - A wide variety of labels for cloth, wood, metal or plastic products.

Leashes or Leads - Cloth, leather or plastic leashes or leads for pets..

Letter Openers - Plastic, metal or wood letter openers.

License Plate Frames - Metal or plastic license plate frames.

Manicure Set - Fingernail file, clippers, polish, etc. in a container..

Match Boxes of Books - Printed match boxes or books.

Magazine Binder - Binder of three hole binder book with hobby name.

Mugs - Drink mugs of metal, plastic or ceramic.

Name Tags - Plastic or leather name tags for luggage, golf and bowling bags, etc.

Napkins - Paper or cloth napkins, napkin holders or napkin rings.

Neck Ties - Ties with embroidered or printed hobby name, logo or emblem.

Needle Point Patterns - Special designed patterns that depict the hobby.

Notebooks - Notebooks of various size with the hobby name, logo or special design.

NotePads or Cards - Printed with a wide variety of hobby related sketches.

Paper Clip Holders - Metal, plastic or ceramic paper clip, pin or rubber band holders.

Pencil Holder - Various pencil holder designs of wood, metal or ceramic.

Pencils or Pens - Produced with hobby name, logo or emblem applied.

Pendants - Metal, ceramic or plastic designed pendants.

Pen Light or Key Chain Light - Produced with hobby name or logo applied.

Photo Albums - Standard photo albums.

Photo Cut-outs - Plastic, metal or wood cut-outs.

Photo Frames - Wood desk or wall photo frames.

Pillows - Decorative and throw-pillows.

Pin Trays - Plastic, wood or ceramic trays to hold pins.

Placemats - fabric, paper or plastic placemats.

Post Cards - A wide variety of post cards depicting the hobby photos or drawings.

Posters - Printed wall posters depicting the hobby by photos or drawings.

Office Kit - Carrying case with tape, paper clips, miniature stapler, rubber bands, etc.

Raincoats - Plastic or waterproof cloth raincoats.

Rings - Metal, ceramic or plastic rings.

Rubber Stamp - Rubber stamp and pad with a variety of designs depicting the hobby.

Rulers - One foot or yardstick measurers of wood or plastic.

Scarves - Woven cloth scarves with hobby name, logo or emblems.

Sewing Kits - Thread, needles, pins, scissors, etc. all in a kit.

Shoe Horn - Ornate plastic, wood or metal shoe horn.

Shoe Laces - Cloth shoe laces with the hobby name or logo.

Shoe Shine Kit - Various shoe polishes, brushes and cloths in a wood or metal box.

Stamp Pads - Ink pad for moistening stamps.

Stationery - A wide range of stationery can be printed with logo or sketches of the hobby.

Stuffed Animals or Characters - These stuffed characters would depict the hobby or interest.

Sweaters - Knitted sweaters with woven in or applied patterns depicting the hobby..

Sun Visors - Plastic or fabric sun visors with the hobby name or logo on the brim.

Tape Measure - Small metal or plastic pocket tape measure.

Tape Recorder - Tapes or small hand held recorders.

Tee Shirts - A wide variety of tee or sweat shirts can be produced with hobby logos or designs

Telephone Pads - Message or note pads.

Thermos - Plastic or metal thermos.

Thermometer - Window, oral or refrigerator thermometers.

Tie Pins - Metal, ceramic or plastic tie pins.

Tie Rack - Wood, metal or plastic tie racks or hangers.

Towels - Hand, bath or beach towels with designs depicting the hobby.

Tote Bags - Cloth carrying bags.

Toothpick Holders - Ceramic, metal or wood containers for toothpicks.

Travel Clocks - Purchased travel clocks with hobby logos or emblems applied.

Travel Kits - Flashlight, flares, jumper cables, etc. in a container.

Umbrellas - Plastic or cloth umbrellas.

Watches - Pocket, pendant or wrist watches with hobby logos or emblems on the face.

Wines - Wines with hobby names, logos or emblems on the label.

Windshield Covers - Heavy paper, cardboard or cloth windshield covers.

APPENDIX C

Listed below are a wide variety of special interest subjects that have related hobby enthusiasts, clubs, organizations, groups or publications related to that particular subject. There are undoubtedly many subjects that we have overlooked, however, this list should help you focus in on your area of interest.

-A-

Accounting
Acrobatics
Acting
Adventure
Advertising
Aerobatics
Aerospace
Aircraft
Airplanes
Ammunition
Animation
Antiques
Autographs
Aquariums
Archery
Architecture
Armor
Art

Astrology
Astronomy
Autobon
Automobiles
Auto Racing
Avionics
Aquariums
Archery
Architecture
Armor
Art
Astrology
Astronomy
Autobon
Autographs
Automobiles
Auto Racing
Avionics

-B-	-C-
Backpacking	Cabinet Making
Baking	Cake Decorating
Ballet	Calligraphy
Ballooning	Cameras
Banks	Camping
Baseball	Canoeing
Baseball Cards	Cards
Basket Weaving	Carousels
Basketball	Cartography
Basketball Cards	Cartooning
Bass Fishing	Carving
Bicycling	Cats
Big Bands	Cattle
Birds	Ceramics
Billiards	Chess
Blacksmith	Cinema
Boat Building	Circuses
Boating	Citizen Band Radio
Boats	Classic Aircraft
Body Building	Classic Autos
Body Surfing	Climbing
Boxing	Clocks
Bowling	Clowns
Bridge	Clothing
Bridges	Coin Collecting
	Cooking

Comedy
Computers
Cosmotology
Country Running
Crafts
Cribbage
Croquet
Cross
Cross Country Skiing
Cycling

-D-
Dancing
Dams
Darts
Decorating
Design
Diet
Dirt Biking
Diving
Dogs
Dog Shows
Dog Training
Dolls
Doll Houses
Dominos
Drama

Drawing
Dressmaking
Driving
Duck Hunting
Dune Buggies

-E-
Earth
Earthquake
Ecology
Economics
Electronics
Emblems
Embroidery
Engineering
Entertainment
Engines
Entomology
Environment
Equestrian
Etching
Evolution
Exercise

-F-
Fabric
Falconry

Farming
Farm Animals
Farm Tools
Fashion
Fashion Design
Fencing
Film
Fine Arts
Fire Arms
Fishing
Flowers
Flower Arrangements
Flying
Food
Football
Footwear
Fraternal Clubs
Furniture Design
Furniture Making

-G-

Games
Gardening
Gemology
Genealogy
Geography
Geology

Glassware
Gliding
Golf
Green Houses
Guitar
Guns
Gymnastics

-H-

Hairdressing
Hang Gliding
Health
Heraldry
History
Hockey
Home Movies
Horses
Horseback Riding
Horseshoes
Horticulture
Humor
Hunting

-I-

Ice Skating
Indian Art
Insects

Interior Design

-J-
Jazz
Jewelry
Jigsaw Puzzles
Jogging
Jokes
Journalism
Judo
Juggling

-K-
Kaleidoscopes
Karate
Kites
Knitting

-L-
Landscaping
Language
Lapidary
Leather Craft
Lighter Than Air

-M-
Macrame
Magazines
Magic
Marksmanship
Mathematics
Medals
Medicine
Microwave
Military Aircraft
Military Warships
Miniatures
Model Airplanes
Model Boats
Model Cars
Model Homes
Model Railroads
Mobile Homes
Mountain Climbing
Motorcycles
Movie Memorabilia
Movies
Music
Music Boxes
Mysteries

-N-
Nature
Nautical
Needlepoint

-O-
Oceanography
Off Road
Oil Painting
Orchestra
Orchids
Ornothology
Outer Space
Out Rigger

-P-
Painting
Photography
Physics
Player Pianos
Poetry
Poker
Politics
Polo
Pool
Pottery
Post Cards

Posters
Prints
Psychic
Puzzles

-Q-
Quilting
Quizzes

-R-
Racing
Race Horses
Racketball
Radio
Railroads
Rappel
Rare Books
Records
Recreational Vehicles
Religions
Reptiles
Romance
Romantic
Rowing
Rug Making
Running

-S-
Sailing
Scouting
Sculling
Sculpturing
Seniors
Sewing
Sheet Music
Shell Collecting
Shooting
Shuffleboard
Singing
Skate Boarding
Skating
Skeet Shooting
Sketching
Skiing
Ski Mobile
Skin Diving
Slot Machines
Soaring
Song Writing
Soccer
Space
Speech
Square Dancing
Stage

Stained Glass
Stamp Collecting
Surfing
Swimming

-T-
Taxidermy
Teddy Bears
Tennis
Theater
Tools
Toys
Track & Field
Trail Bikes
Trailer
Trains
Travel
Travel
Trucks

-U-
Ultralites
Underwater
Unlueuse

-V-
Vacation

Vending Machines
Veterans
Video
Victrollas
Voice
Volleyball

-W-
Walking
Watercolors
Water Polo
Water Skiing
Weapons
Weaving
Weight Lifting
Whistling
Whittling
Wind Surfing
Wine
Wood Carving
Woodworking
Wrestling
Writing

-Y-
Yachting
Yacht Racing

INDEX

NOTES

NOTES

NOTES

NOTES

NOTES

NOTES